This book is a beautiful illustration of the loving transformation that God can work in our lives. Nicki's story has deeply moved me as she has so courageously allowed the reader into her world, and by doing so challenges each one of us to trust and hope.
Clare Lambert, church ministry leader

This is an easy-to-read, honest and thoughtful account of Nicki's journey from feeling 'less than ordinary' to feeling valued and worthy. Many women will relate to Nicki's feelings, and this book is a real encouragement to all, that with God's help and good friends we can become the person God wants us to be.
Gill Barden, physiotherapist

The author's humble and open heart is spilled out on every page as she openly shares her own insecurities. It's refreshing, honest and real and includes scriptural encouragement. It will build up your heart and help you learn to love yourself.
Caroline Gillespie, full-time mum

Aren't we good at hiding our real selves?
Do you yearn for deeper and more trustworthy relationships, yet suffer from the pain of low self-esteem?
This book is refreshingly honest and offers practical advice and wisdom to help reassure us that God has made us special and unique.
Helen Parry Burns, Charity Accountant

G000146550

Less than ordinary?

My journey into finding my true self

Nicki Copeland

instant
ap stle

First published in Great Britain in 2013

Instant Apostle
The Hub
3-5 Rickmansworth Road
Watford
Herts
WD18 0GX

Unless otherwise identified, all biblical quotations are taken from the Holy Bible, New International Version® Anglicized, NIV® Copyright © 1979, 1984, 2011 by http://www.biblica.com/ Biblica, Inc. Used by permission. All rights reserved worldwide.

Every effort has been made to seek permission to use copyright material reproduced in this book. The publisher apologises for those cases where permission might not have been sought and, if notified, will formally seek permission at the earliest opportunity.

The views and opinions expressed in this work are those of the author and do not necessarily reflect the views and opinions of the publisher.

British Library Cataloguing-in-Publication Data

A catalogue record for this book is available from the British Library

This book and all other Instant Apostle books are available from Instant Apostle:

Website: www.instantapostle.com
E-mail: info@instantapostle.com

ISBN 978-1-909728-00-4

Printed in Great Britain

Instant Apostle is a new way of getting ideas flowing, between followers of Jesus, and between those who would like to know more about His Kingdom.

It's not just about books and it's not about a one-way information flow. It's about building a community where ideas are exchanged. Ideas will be expressed at an appropriate length. Some will take the form of books. But in many cases ideas can be expressed more briefly than in a book. Short books, or pamphlets, will be an important part of what we provide. As with pamphlets of old, these are likely to be opinionated, and produced quickly so that the community can discuss them.

Well-known authors are welcome, but we also welcome new writers. We are looking for prophetic voices, authentic and original ideas, produced at any length; quick and relevant, insightful and opinionated. And as the name implies, these will be released very quickly, either as Kindle books or printed texts or both.

Join the community. Get reading, get writing and get discussing!

Acknowledgements

First and foremost my thanks go to God, for loving me unconditionally, for being so patient with me and for gently and firmly guiding me along Your path. Thank You too for the many blessings You continue to pour into my life.

To my Pete. What can I say? You are always there for me, loving me, supporting me and encouraging me. I am so blessed to be your wife, and I thank God for bringing you into my life. Thank you for giving me the time to write, for encouraging me to follow my dreams, and for your patience in reading endless drafts! You truly are the wind beneath my wings, and I love you.

To Alex, Andrew and Emily. It's such a privilege to be your mum. You have taught me so much over the years, and I am very proud of you. I love you so much.

To my parents. Thank you for always loving me, for always being there for me when I needed you, and for everything you have taught me over the years.

To my family and friends. Thank you for loving me for who I am, for encouraging me to believe in myself, and for sticking by me through the good times and the bad.

To Manoj, who pushed me to dig deep and write about my journey. I may not have thanked you for it at the time, but I am very grateful!

And finally, but by no means least, to everyone I have known over the years who has had an impact on my life and who has contributed to making me the person I am today.

Nicki Copeland can be contacted via her website www.nickicopeland.co.uk

Contents

Foreword

Recently I heard someone say this: 'It's not until you take a risk that you make a connection.' Many people would say that it's only once you've made a connection that you will take a risk, but probably the opposite is true.

When we take a risk, all kinds of possibilities open up. Maybe we decide to speak out in a meeting when we'd prefer to stay silent and we find that what we said is significant in bringing change. Or perhaps someone wrongs us but we choose to let it pass and we find that our silence has more of an impact on those who noticed it than our reacting would ever have done. There are many ways of taking relational risks, and when we do, we usually find that we change and grow, and so do our relationships.

Taking a risk means choosing to do something different from what we naturally want to do, and it often involves stepping into the unknown because we don't know what the outcome will be. Nicki, in writing this book, has taken a risk. It is one of many that she has taken in her life. Some of them she writes about, with great honesty, in these pages. In doing so she demonstrates her courage in facing some of the aspects of her personality that once hindered her and would have continued to do so had she not first faced them and then braved writing about them here.

It has been a pleasure for me to get to know Nicki in the past year or so, and since doing so I've formed the impression of a woman who is self-confident, quietly sure of her strengths, determined to achieve what she embarks on and someone with good people skills, sensitivity to the needs of those around her and a desire to empower others as well as find empowerment for herself. All of this is a far cry from the person she describes herself as in the first part of the book. She is a testimony of what God can do in a person's life when they surrender themselves to Him and seek His will for their life.

As you read what she has written, you'll discover as I have that Nicki is no ordinary woman!

Lindsay Melluish, Regional Leader, New Wine London & South East; Associate Pastor, St Paul's Ealing

Introduction

When I started writing this book, it was intended to be a book about communication and how we can use it to make our relationships as good as they can possibly be. But as time went on, I was taken on a journey through my own relationships over the course of my life, and I realised that for a long time, there had been a vital piece missing.

For much of my life I struggled with relationships and found it hard to make friends. I had a few friends, but none that were really close, and I figured it must be because I wasn't special enough. So I found myself either trying to change who I was so people would like me, or I hid myself away, feeling that if I allowed the real 'me' to be on show, I would either be mocked or no one would want to know me.

As I grew older, I figured that if people wouldn't like me for my personality, maybe they would accept me for my achievements. I embraced perfectionism and worked hard in school and at college, thinking that perhaps I could find an identity that way.

After completing my A levels I found a job as a secretary at a publishing house in London, and I was there for a little more than a year before the company moved to Oxford and made me redundant. I enjoyed the job, but I never really felt that I fitted in with my colleagues. I worked hard and my boss was pleased with my work, so in my mind this concreted my reasoning that even if I wasn't much liked, I could be accepted if I worked hard.

This pattern followed me for many years. I didn't realise that my fundamental mistake was that I had never accepted myself for who I really was. I tried so hard to be someone I thought people would like that I no longer knew who the real me was inside. I was desperate to feel loved and accepted, but I didn't understand that I was preventing this from happening because I didn't love and accept myself.

This book is about my journey into self-acceptance, into learning to love myself, and into becoming the person I was created to be. It is about embracing my uniqueness and seeing this as a strength, rather than wishing I was like everybody else. It is about enjoying being who I am, and understanding that my journey is not the same as anybody else's. It is about my growing self-confidence as I accept that I do have something to contribute to the world around me and to the lives of those I have the privilege of knowing. It is about understanding that there is a plan for my life that I have been uniquely equipped to fulfil, and it is about the excitement of seeing that plan unfold!

I guess before we go any further I ought to tell you who I am. I'm a middle-aged woman, I am married with three children, I work as a freelance copywriter, editor and proofreader, I am a part-time Theology student, and I am a Christian. I believe that we have all been created by God, that He loves us passionately and that He has a plan for each of our lives. I believe God wants us to be happy, but I also believe that life isn't easy, and I have had my share of struggles. But I know that my faith has given me the strength to get through these times when I know I wouldn't have been able to cope on my own.

Chapter 1
Less than ordinary?

My relationships, with God and with those around me, are the most important things in my life. Without God, my family and my friends, my life would be empty. My work is important to me, and so are all the other things I do, but without relationships, what would I be working for?

Money, possessions, a nice house, and so on, are of limited value without anyone to share them with. Even those of us who live alone share our lives with friends and relatives, even if we don't see them every day.

As I look back over my life, I can see how my relationships have been developing over the years. To be honest, relationships were always something I found difficult. I found it hard to trust people and to 'let them in', partly because I didn't think I had anything interesting to offer, and partly because I was afraid of being rejected. So I hid myself away. I lacked confidence, I felt that I had very little to give and, if I'm brutally honest, I didn't like myself much as a person and didn't see why anyone else should like me either. I considered myself to be inferior to everyone else – to be 'less than ordinary'.

Over recent years I've been learning that the starting point for any relationship with another person is my relationship with myself. I am realising that I have to learn to accept myself for who I am before I can enjoy relationships of any real depth. This isn't an easy lesson to learn.

I am learning that if I don't love and accept myself, it is very difficult to have meaningful relationships with other people. Yes, I can have relationships, and there are many people over the years that I have had, and still have, the privilege of calling friends. But, because of my inability to put my real self 'out there', many of these relationships were superficial. There was always an internal struggle going on. I would think, 'Why should this person like me when I'm not likable? Why would anyone love me when I'm not lovable?'

Self-fulfilling prophecy?

Feeling unlovable can make different people act in different ways but, more often than not, I believe it results in behaviour that ends up pushing people away, and it becomes a self-fulfilling prophecy. I have experienced this many times. I haven't felt lovable or worthy of someone's friendship so I have kept them at arm's length and made them think I wasn't interested in friendship.

I know this to be true. I was chatting recently with someone who is now one of my closest friends, and this very subject came up. She explained how when she first met me she got the impression that I just wasn't interested in developing a relationship with her, even though she was trying to be my friend. Yet the reality couldn't have been further from the truth! I desperately wanted to be her friend, but I couldn't get past the blockage. It was a very painful place to be in.

When we lack self-acceptance, whatever our behaviour pattern might be, when a person leaves us or a friendship breaks down, it just confirms our perceived notion that we are unlovable. As I look back, I can see many other times when this has happened to me because I didn't let people in. I didn't do it consciously, but there has definitely been a pattern of keeping people at arm's length and then allowing this to confirm my negative beliefs about myself. Even though I craved love and acceptance, because I couldn't love and accept myself, I couldn't allow myself to receive love and acceptance from anyone else.

Another thing I would do would be to misinterpret things that people said, or try to analyse what they said, looking for a hidden meaning. I would find hidden implications that, in reality, weren't there. I found it very difficult to accept a compliment and would think that the person paying it was just trying to be nice because they thought they ought to be – or perhaps they were just being polite – but that they didn't really mean it.

My self-confidence was also very low. I greatly feared failure, to the point where I wouldn't do anything unless I was absolutely sure I would succeed. Failure would leave me feeling even more useless, and even more unworthy of people's friendship and attention. I would put such pressure on myself to always get things right, to never make a mistake, because I thought people would think less of me and consider that I wasn't worth knowing.

Over the course of time, a number of things have happened in my life that are helping me to break this cycle. Very slowly I began to wonder why I struggled to believe what people said to me. Gradually I began to consider whether, when I was paid a compliment, the person might really mean what they said and wasn't just being polite. As I looked deeper and tried to analyse what people said, there were times when I realised that the person hadn't been obliged to say what they had said; they hadn't been cornered and left with no option but to say something nice, so perhaps they did mean it after all. I also became better at 'reading' people and being able to work out whether or not I thought they were being genuine. I didn't always get it right, and I still don't, but I began to be able to sense whether people were being sincere or not.

I began to dare to think about the possibility that I might actually be an okay kind of person, and to wonder whether I could possibly take the risk and start to open myself up to people. I started to understand that I could take people at face value, that there wasn't always a hidden agenda, that they weren't all waiting to trip me up and make me look daft.

I started to realise that I had to make a conscious decision to look at things differently. It was very hard, almost like retraining my mind to a new way of thinking, and it took a long time – indeed, it is an ongoing process. Sometimes I feel as though I am fighting against my instincts, but these instincts are based on my perceptions, and I know that my perceptions are sometimes wrong.

As I look back, I realise that I have spent much of my life trying to please everyone around me and conforming to expected patterns of behaviour. I guess it was easier for me to conform to these patterns and the expectations that were upon me than to try to assert who I really was. Perhaps I didn't really know who I was until I started to question why I did things in the way I did them, and began to question my automatic responses to situations and events in my life.

Baby steps

This has been a long and difficult journey for me; indeed, it's a road I am still travelling, and am likely to be travelling for the rest of my life. I realise that I still have a long way to go, but I have begun to be able to accept myself for who I am and am beginning to believe in myself. I have even begun to like who I am and to enjoy being me.

I am able to accept that I am made to be unique, and that the fact that there is no one else like me on the face of the earth might actually be a positive thing because it means I am special! I am realising that without self-acceptance, I could never be happy; I would always be dissatisfied with who I am. Without self-belief, I could never achieve my potential.

Once we begin to accept ourselves for who we are, and start to enjoy becoming the person we were created to be, it becomes easier to form meaningful relationships.

In the time I have spent looking back over my life and thinking about who I am, I have been examining the behaviours that are natural to my personality and those that I have learned. There are some things I don't like very much about myself, and I'm working on those. The difference now is that I am able to admit my shortcomings, to myself and to others; previously I thought that to admit my faults would push people away because it would make them realise what a horrible person I really am. I now realise that (most) people are actually quite accepting, and very often are fighting the same battles themselves. It's actually very reassuring to realise that I'm not the only person facing particular problems or difficulties!

All these things have a bearing on how I relate to other people. I am finding that as I begin to be more open about who I am, about the struggles I face as well as the blessings in my life, sometimes people open up to me and talk about their own struggles and difficulties. This creates bonds, and these bonds grow stronger as we talk more and get to know each other better.

It is very difficult to be really open with someone when we are not used to doing it. I found it really hard, and it left me feeling very vulnerable. For this reason I was very careful who I chose to talk to. I made sure that I opened up to someone who I thought would be trustworthy – I had to be pretty sure that my trust wouldn't be betrayed. If we open up to someone who betrays our trust, this leaves us feeling violated, and makes it ten times as hard to do it again.

While we can never be 100 per cent sure about anybody, we can look for 'clues' as to how we think people might treat our confidences. We can test the water with small things and observe their reactions to what we say. We can observe how they interact with other people, and whether or not other people appear to trust them. And we can listen to what they talk about: if they are gossiping about other people, we need to keep our secrets to ourselves!

I also think it is a good idea to think carefully about what we choose to share. When I started to open up to people, I began by sharing something that was personal but that wouldn't have been seriously detrimental to me if the confidence had been broken. Sharing our deepest, darkest secrets the first time we talk with someone is not to be advised! In this way, we slowly build trust, and as the person keeps our confidence, we will feel more able to share deeper things, if we choose to, as time goes on.

As we open up to people, we may well find that they open up to us, too, and share personal things with us. In turn, we will be responsible for keeping the confidences entrusted to us. This mutual trust is vital, and will grow as the relationship deepens. Without trust, I believe relationships cannot go beyond a superficial level. Betrayal of trust does much damage, not only to relationships, but to people as well.

Chapter 2
Who am I really?

I believe we are all made to be unique, with different gifts, different abilities and different interests. If we were all the same, the world would be a much poorer place. If everyone were great with numbers, for example, we'd have a glut of accountants and financial advisers, but no one would need advice. Neither would there be anyone to build or maintain our houses. If everyone were artistic, the world would be beautiful, but I very much doubt whether it would be functional. Beauty and art are essential, but we need the practical too.

I remember going to a business networking meeting a few years ago. There were a lot less people there than had been expected – probably only around a dozen of us in total – and because we were so few, we sat in a circle to introduce ourselves to one another. I remember trying to stifle my amusement as the majority of the people introduced themselves as a financial advisor or a business development consultant. Clearly, none of them were going to obtain much new business from that meeting! I didn't obtain any new clients either, but at least I could introduce myself as something other than a financial advisor or a business consultant!

To me, our differences are a part of the beauty of the world. Meeting new people and discovering who they are and what they are good at is fascinating. I still find it quite difficult to talk to people I don't know – I always fear that they aren't going to like me – but I'm getting better at it, and I am learning from experience that what I am likely to gain from the relationship far outweighs any risk or discomfort I might feel at the beginning. Depending on the context of the meeting, I look for things we might have in common and build from there. I realise too that, more often than not, the other person is feeling just as nervous as I am!

It's also very exciting to watch our children grow up and discover their own talents and giftings. I have three children and they are all very different. One of my sons is gifted technologically, the other is a talented cook, and my daughter is very creative and imaginative. As a parent, it is extremely rewarding to see their abilities develop and to watch them mature. If they were all to grow up to be the same, I think we and the world would be missing out.

My children's diversity also helps the household: everyone contributes something different, and all contributions are valued. Whether it's fixing the internet when it crashes, cooking lovely dinners or cakes, or producing pretty pictures for the walls, everyone's input is welcomed and appreciated. Having different strengths and abilities also helps them to feel valued for who they are as individuals, and to know that they are unique and special, and they all know that they are valued not just by their family, but by others too.

I think it is important to embrace our giftings. I have noticed that when we are good at something, we are more likely to enjoy doing it. I have never been good at drawing; consequently I really don't enjoy doing it at all and try to avoid it if at all possible! On the other hand, I have always loved reading. Spotting a number of errors in a book some years ago, which spoilt my enjoyment of what was otherwise a very interesting biography, made me pursue the possibility of becoming a proofreader and editor – a job I now love.

What makes us who we are?

As well as different gifts, abilities and interests, we all have different personalities, and we all relate to each other in different ways. In the broadest terms, everyone falls somewhere along the extrovert–introvert scale. Some are extreme extroverts, some are extreme introverts, and some fall somewhere in the middle. I believe most of us have both tendencies in different areas of our lives, although we probably fall closer to one end of the scale or the other.

Much of our behaviour is instinctive and results from our personality type, our beliefs and values, our life experiences and our emotions. These factors determine who we are, and who we are determines how we respond or react to people and situations, and how we communicate with others.

Forthright people will be direct and to the point. They have little time for small talk – they'll just cut to the chase and say what's on their mind. On the other hand, people of a more timid nature might skirt around the issue at hand, particularly if they are uncomfortable with the topic. They may take pains to avoid the issue altogether, and perhaps will even try to steer clear of a particular person if they feel uncomfortable around them.

People of opposite natures like this could well find it difficult to communicate with each other. The forthright person is likely to get frustrated with the timid person, perhaps feeling that they never receive a straight answer and that they are unable to have a frank, open discussion. The timid person may well feel intimidated by the forthright person. This in turn may make them more tongue-tied as they worry about the reaction they will receive to anything they might say.

Our emotions, too, play a huge part in the way we relate to other people, and we communicate differently according to how we feel at the time. Joy and excitement will probably make us talk a lot more, for example. Anger might lead us to say things we don't mean and later regret.

Fear motivates people in different ways. Some people come out fighting, on the basis that attack is the best form of defence. The problem with this is that people can come across as aggressive and will sometimes cause offence.

Some people hide behind humour and say something funny to break the ice. This is great, but they must be careful that they don't end up with only superficial relationships. Others hide behind lies because they can't face the truth, either about the situation or about themselves, so they fabricate something or make themselves out to be someone that they think will be more acceptable to the person they are talking to. Still others just become very indecisive – they don't know what to say or do, so they end up saying or doing nothing.

In terms of my own personality, I am naturally an introvert; I am quite sensitive, both to my own and to other people's feelings; I am a perfectionist and I have an over-active conscience! This means I worry greatly about upsetting or offending people and feel absolutely awful for days if I think I have done or said anything to hurt someone else.

I have always struggled with self-confidence, and one of my biggest fears has always been that I wouldn't be accepted and liked for who I am. This made me one of those timid and indecisive people I mentioned earlier. In many situations I wouldn't know what to say, and didn't feel I had anything valuable to contribute to the conversation, so I would end up saying nothing. I am aware now that because of this, at times I would come across to other people as unfriendly, stand-offish even, but fear was controlling my behaviour and I didn't have any confidence in myself to behave any differently.

As a child I was painfully shy, especially at school. Somehow I felt that I didn't really fit in, and I didn't have any particularly close friends. It didn't help that in my first year or so at school the two close friends I had made moved away. I made a couple of other friends during my primary school years, but these friendships didn't last either. One of them stole my favourite pen from me, and I was separated from the other when our classes were shuffled at the end of one of the academic years. After this, I never really made any more close friends.

These experiences left me feeling that if I made friends I was leaving myself open to being hurt. So I learned to withdraw and hide.

Perhaps my shyness, coupled with this fear of being hurt, meant that I was communicating non-verbally that I wasn't interested in friendship. Children are very perceptive, and if I was giving off these signals, maybe it's not surprising that other children gave up on me.

Because even from an early age I never experienced lasting or close friendships, I reasoned that it was probably because I wasn't particularly likeable, not especially fun to be around, and that the people who did spend time with me were tolerating me rather than really wanting to be with me and be my friend.

This pattern continued into high school. None of my friends from primary school went to the same high school as I did so I had to start over and attempt to form new friendships. I made a few friends, but none that were particularly close, as they all seemed to already have their own best friend. I wasn't one of the 'cool' crowd, and I often felt that I was laughed at by those who were 'in'.

I was amazed when, a number of years ago, someone contacted me through the website 'Friends reunited' and said that at school he had always admired the way I had been true to who I was and hadn't tried to change in order to be accepted. I was amazed by this, as this particular person had been one of the 'in' crowd, and I naturally assumed that he shared the same opinion as everyone else and thought I was a loser. It just goes to show that our perceptions of what people are really thinking can be so wrong!

As a teenager, I was asked out on a date a couple of times by boys at school. I have no idea how they even got to the stage of asking me out because I was so shy, but they did! I accepted, but was very nervous. In fact, I was so nervous that when the occasions arrived, I was so tongue-tied that I barely said a word the whole time! Needless to say, there was no second date on either occasion! I must have been very hard work for those poor boys!

Zero confidence

When my confidence was at rock bottom, I would blame myself for everything that went wrong around me, even if it wasn't my fault. Because I am a perfectionist, I felt that nothing I ever did was good enough. I always thought that whatever I chose to do, someone else would be able to do it better than I could, and that my efforts were mediocre at best. This affected everything – my work, my homemaking skills, my cooking, my driving...

As a child I had music lessons. I loved music and singing (I still do), and I had piano and oboe lessons. But I didn't practise enough. The reason, I realise now, is that I didn't want anyone to hear me making mistakes. I recognise now how ridiculous that is, but that's how deeply my fears ran. Obviously I didn't progress particularly far with either of these instruments, and I now wish that I had persevered and that I had had the confidence to practise, no matter who might have been listening. I would love to take up the oboe again one day, when I have some more free time. Who knows, maybe one day...

In every situation I would always do what I thought was expected of me in order to be accepted or to obtain approval. I had little confidence in anything that I did, and I certainly wouldn't do anything that would be considered to be 'outside the box'. How many work appraisals did I have over the years that suggested I should try to show more initiative?! Far too many! But I didn't have the confidence, in case I did something wrong.

I wouldn't attempt anything new, and I found it incredibly hard to show anyone anything I had done because I thought they would think it was rubbish. I realise now that this wasn't true, but it was how I felt at the time about almost everything I did.

Unless I was completely sure that I could do it, I would try to avoid doing anything 'public' as I felt I would be opening myself up to criticism, which I wouldn't be able to cope with as I would take it as a personal rejection.

I occasionally did readings out loud in church, partly because my father encouraged me and coached me, and partly because, as I said earlier, I loved reading and it was one thing I was reasonably confident of my ability in. I remember one Sunday morning when I was about to do a reading in the service, I tripped over as I was stepping up onto the platform. I was mortified. How I managed to carry on, I don't know. I think I only managed because the sense of failure I would have had at not carrying out my task would have been worse than the embarrassment I already felt. The fact that my dad was on the platform at the time helped too, and the knowledge that I had his love and support. But I think my face was probably extremely red during the entire reading!

Observing from the outside

It wasn't until these patterns of behaviour were pointed out to me that I realised what I was doing. They were so deeply ingrained in me that they had become completely natural. Now that I am becoming increasingly aware of them, though, I try to evaluate situations more objectively.

If something goes wrong, I try to look more impartially at what has happened. This is not so that I can apportion blame – that doesn't help anyone – but it can be helpful sometimes to understand what went wrong so that things can be done differently in the future. If it was my fault I will accept the responsibility and try to put things right. But I am also learning to stand up for myself, and if I think I am being accused of something unjustly, I will say so!

This is a long and hard lesson to learn, and I still find myself apologising at times when I shouldn't, when I haven't done anything that I ought to be apologising for. If someone knocks into my trolley in the supermarket, why am I the one who says sorry?! I am still learning the difference between taking responsibility for something I've done wrong and shouldering the blame for problems that are not of my making. As I say, it's a slow process, but I'm getting there.

My instinctive reaction when I feel called to do something out of my comfort zone is very often still that I can't do it, that I'm not capable, that there are thousands of people who would be able to do it far better than I would – why me? But over time I've slowly been realising that I *am* capable, and that actually my efforts *are* good enough. I'm also beginning to understand that, sometimes, a little less than perfect is entirely acceptable – sometimes 'good enough' is good enough. I'm learning not to hide, and am gaining confidence to put myself 'on show', to take the risk of making a mistake, or even of failing altogether.

How much my fears were a natural part of my personality and how much was learned over the years I have no idea. We could get into the nature versus nurture discussion here, but I don't know the answers. I guess it's probably a bit of both. But the good news is that I have begun to understand and accept that I am uniquely made, and that there are some things that I am uniquely equipped to do.

Over the years, my self-confidence has grown, and I am no longer tongue-tied and driven by fear. Indeed, some would say I now talk too much (and they're probably right)! There are still occasions when I feel out of my depth in a conversation, but at those times I try to listen and learn, and just hope that no one asks for my opinion on the matter!

The fact that this book is in your hands is testament to how far I've come. I distinctly remember the feeling of panic welling up inside when I was given the task of writing a story in primary school. If I had to write a story for homework I simply couldn't do it, and somehow I managed to get away with not giving my exercise book in! I'm amazed that the teacher didn't realise (or perhaps she did and for whatever reason didn't follow it up)!

It became easier in high school when I had to write essays for English and other subjects. I still struggled a little, but I think because I was able to be more objective, and knew roughly what the teacher was looking for in terms of an answer to the question, it was easier. In these instances there were clear boundaries to which I could conform, and there was a limit to how much of my personality I had to pour into these assignments. But there was no way I could write a story from my imagination – that would be giving too much of myself away, and opening myself up for criticism or rejection.

When I started work, I sometimes had to write letters, either on my own behalf or on behalf of the people I was working for. This was something else I found very difficult – what if I made a mistake and included incorrect information? What if I phrased it badly? Gradually, though, over time, this became easier, as what I had written was usually accepted without question. I was also very fortunate to work with really nice people who didn't make me feel as though it was a personal criticism if they thought something I had written ought to be changed.

When I started writing this book, I found it incredibly hard to show anyone anything I had written. The fear of rejection was immense. Somehow, though, I just knew that this message on my heart was important and that I needed to share it, and I fought the instinct to hide away.

As I talk to people about my experiences and difficulties, I discover that many people struggle with the same issues that I struggle with. Now that I am learning to fight back, I felt that I had to share my story in the hope that it will inspire others to feel that they can fight back too, and to understand that each one of us is uniquely made and has a valuable contribution to make.

There are very few people who are called to try to change the whole world, but I believe we can all make a big difference in our small corner of it.

Chapter 3
Journeying into self-acceptance

So what has changed? How did I manage to begin to change my way of thinking and set out on the long road to self-acceptance?

It all came to a head on a church holiday some years ago. We were staying in a beautiful converted castle in Derbyshire. During the day times we would go sightseeing or do other activities, and after dinner we had short teaching sessions before relaxing together for the evening. These teaching sessions over the course of the week were on the subject of 'authentic relationships'.

During one of the sessions I remember breaking down in tears because I felt that I didn't have any of these real relationships, and I desperately wanted them. I had a long chat with two girl friends and was finally able to open up and explain how I felt – that I thought people tolerated me and didn't really like me, that I had nothing to offer, that I was boring, no fun to be around, and so on. They appeared to be quite shocked, and that in turn shocked me! They didn't understand why I felt that way and gently reassured me that they really did like me for who I was and really enjoyed being my friend. I don't know how, but somehow I knew they were being genuine.

Once I'd got over the shock that maybe some people actually did like me for who I really was, and they weren't just putting up with me because they were Christians and were being nice, my relationships with these girls, and a few others, began to grow. Once I learnt how to let them in, I experienced a depth of relationships that I had never known existed.

This was very difficult to begin with, and I think with every two steps forwards I must have taken at least one step backwards. It's incredibly hard to change habits that have been ingrained since childhood and that have been compounded over many years. When you have struggled all your life to feel accepted, and live in constant fear of rejection, allowing people in to see the real person inside doesn't come easily.

As I started to open up to people, though, I discovered a freedom in trusting. My confidence very slowly began to grow, and my fear of making mistakes began to subside, although it would still be many years before I got to the point where I wouldn't tear myself to pieces if I got something wrong! Even now, depending what I get wrong, I am often still very hard on myself if I mess up.

I now count these girls as among my closest friends. I love them dearly and am eternally grateful both to them and to God for making them a part of my life. I owe them more than they will ever realise.

During this process, at times it almost felt as though I was stepping out on to a rickety bridge, and I had to rely on others to make sure it didn't give way underneath me. Giving away control, such as it was, and learning to trust other people was a huge step that took real faith and tremendous courage. But it's one that I don't for a single moment regret. The joy of knowing real relationships, of being free to be myself, of knowing I am loved for who I am, warts and all, is truly wonderful.

With these people around me, during the times when it felt as though my whole life was falling apart, I didn't have to pretend that all was going well and that everything in the garden was rosy. These were times when I needed to be able to acknowledge that the roses have thorns. Being able to express honestly what I was going through and how I felt was an important part of the healing process for me. Allowing people to support me, emotionally and practically, was difficult, but very necessary.

Does any of this sound familiar? If so, I would encourage you to look for someone you feel you can trust and start to open up a little. Take it slowly, one step at a time, to allow time for your confidence and trust in each other to build. I know it's not easy – take it from someone who knows – but I honestly believe it will be worth it in the end.

Learning to laugh at myself

As I said earlier, I am a perfectionist. Fear of failure has always been a huge motivator for me. Making mistakes would be a major trauma, and if I failed an exam, well, I would beat myself up for weeks.

Over time, though, and as my self-confidence began to grow, I started to realise that the odd tiny error here and there wasn't going to be life threatening, for me or anyone else. But it wasn't an easy learning experience.

In recent years I worked part-time in the church office, and when I started the job I had to learn not to keep beating myself up when I made a mistake. In many ways it was a 'hidden' job – working behind the scenes, making sure everything functioned well, staying in the background. I was pretty invisible most of the time, and that suited me very well! But one or two aspects were highly visible.

One of these was the Sunday news sheet which was given to everyone as they came in for the service each week. I did my best, but it was inevitable that errors would occasionally slip through. The first time this happened I was mortified. How could I have let it happen? What will people think of me now? They'll think I'm useless at my job, that I can't even get a date right, or spell this word right. One or two people even took the trouble to point the errors out to me. I know they were being kind, but it made me feel even worse!

After this had happened a couple of times, though, and I hadn't got the sack, the church building hadn't fallen down and nobody had resigned their membership over the errors, I began to realise that actually it really wasn't that big a deal. I began to understand that people were far more forgiving of me than I was of myself. Indeed, most people probably didn't even notice the mistake, and if they did, they weren't particularly bothered by it, and they would more than likely forget about it as soon as they put the news sheet down anyway.

I came to accept that none of us is perfect – we all make mistakes – and if anyone really wanted to give me a hard time about such a small error, then maybe that was actually more their problem than mine.

Gradually I began to be more laid back about my slip-ups, and even learnt to laugh about them. When a minor error was pointed out to me, I graciously thanked the person concerned, made a mental note to try not to do it again and filed it in the compartment of my brain marked 'delete'. I had to make a conscious decision to do this, because the temptation to let it eat away at me was too strong otherwise, and I realised that that would only do damage to me. Very occasionally, however, it was an important error, and it would have to be announced in the service that there was a mistake on the news sheet. Yes it was embarrassing, but I learnt to chalk it up to experience and move on. I made a conscious decision not to let it undermine me, my role or my confidence.

My instinct is still to be very hard on myself if I make a mistake. But I'm learning to keep it in perspective. The way I have learnt to deal with it is to make myself think about what the consequences of my error might be. If it's not life changing or detrimental to anyone, I make a conscious decision to once again file it in the 'delete' compartment and move on.

If, on the other hand, there are consequences, however serious, it is important that I take responsibility for my actions, and I take every step I can to put things right and to try to limit and repair the damage. Once I have done all I can, I then do my best to put it behind me. It can be hard, especially if I know I've hurt someone or cost them in terms of time, money or effort, but as I said before, people are gracious and forgiving. The hardest part is forgiving myself, but I'm slowly getting better at that too.

Part of this process is learning to laugh at myself and my mistakes, and not always to take myself seriously. My struggle for self-acceptance meant I really took it to heart if I said or did anything daft, because I thought people would think I was silly, or worse, and would reject me personally. I realise now that at times others must have walked on eggshells around me so as not to risk upsetting me.

It's a good thing to be able to have a laugh at my own expense – it eases tension and breaks the ice – and these days I'm a lot less sensitive. I know now that people won't push me away whenever I drop a clanger, and I often have a good laugh when I make a mistake!

Assertiveness

A long time ago I worked with a man who, personally, was lovely, but professionally I struggled with. Outside of work I got on very well with him: he was great fun, entertaining, and he told many great stories, but if I wasn't careful in the office I could find myself doing more work than was my fair share. We were complete opposites: he was an extrovert and a 'big picture' person who didn't like dealing with small details. I was a quiet introvert who happily managed the details, and who was anxious to please.

He needed some help a couple of times, so naturally I helped him out. But rather than him then taking back the responsibility for these small tasks, somehow they kept ending up on my desk. After a while I felt that he was taking advantage of me, and this began to irritate me, and it began to affect our working relationship.

In the end, I learnt how to be assertive with this man. When he came to ask me for help, I plucked up the courage to tell him gently but firmly what he needed to do rather than taking the hint and letting him take the easy way out! This didn't come naturally to me, and I felt quite guilty about it at times, but I reminded myself that not only did he get paid a lot more than I did, it was his job anyway!

He soon realised that I wasn't going to be a pushover any more, and our working relationship greatly improved after that. I no longer felt resentful at being put upon, and he learnt to respect the boundaries.

A good tip I have picked up on being assertive is to reflect back what the other person is saying, so they know that they have been heard and understood, and then to follow it by putting across my own point of view and the reasons for it, if an explanation is deemed to be necessary, clearly and succinctly. The word 'however' is a very useful one in this situation.

I'm also learning that it's okay to say 'No' sometimes. I have a tendency to automatically consider that other people's needs are more important than my own. Consequently I have found myself totally exhausted at times because I've taken on too much. I'm realising that there are times when it's perfectly acceptable to put my own needs first and to say, 'Sorry, but I can't do it,' or, 'I can't today but I'll be able to help you tomorrow.'

Of course, I will always help people out if I can, especially if they really are in a difficult situation and it's within my ability to help ease the load, but very often there is someone else who can help instead if I am unable to. I still feel very guilty about saying 'No', though, because I feel that I am causing someone else extra trouble, but I know that sometimes I have to be strict with myself, for my own sake and the sake of my family.

Managing conflict

I think it is important that we realise and accept that we won't always agree with one another on every issue. We can 'agree to disagree'. Depending what the issue is, we should be able to respect each other's opinions and carry on as normal. Danger arises, though, when it's a fundamental thing, a big issue that becomes an elephant in the room.

The way we disagree with each other is very important. Strong reactions can result in arguments and shouting matches. Arguments can be very damaging. I would always recommend trying to talk things through calmly rather than losing our temper – certainly this is my preferred way of dealing with disagreements. Some people lose control of their tongue during arguments, and words cannot be taken back once they have been spoken.

I realise that there are some people who actually enjoy a good argument; indeed, some people believe their relationship is healthier for the odd argument now and again as it helps to clear the air. Whatever our preferred way of dealing with conflict, I would say it is essential always to consider the personality and preference of the person we are in conflict with, and to exercise great self-control.

We need to be aware, too, that it isn't always necessary to be proven to be right. We need to have the grace to admit when we are wrong, and to apologise. This can be difficult to do, but it is important in order to repair any damage and to build on the foundation of trust.

I believe it is just as important to apologise to our children when we get it wrong (and we all do!), and to model humility to them in this way. They will discover sooner or later anyway that we are not perfect and that we are not always right. I would much prefer my children to realise now that I get it wrong sometimes, and it is important to me that they have the courage to question me when they disagree with me.

My children's opinions are very important to me; they see things from a very different perspective, and it is really good to talk things through so that I can understand both where they are coming from and why they think in the way they do. As they experience me listening to them and respecting their viewpoint, in turn they will (usually!) listen to me and respect my opinion, too. Normally we are able come to an understanding and resolve the situation without me having to put my foot down, because, having discussed the issue together, they are able to understand the reasons for my decision. At times, they have managed to convince me to change my mind too!

Lessons from parenthood

One of the things that helped my self-confidence to grow was becoming a mum. I think motherhood brought out aspects of my personality that had been deeply buried until then. I knew that if I didn't stand up for my children, no one else would, and needing to be there for them helped me to become more assertive. If I didn't teach my children how to respond to and interact with people, who would? I had to set them a good example.

This made me evaluate the way I chose to live my life and really think about the values I wanted my children to grow up with. What was important to me? What did I want to teach them? What was, what is, the best way to do this? Do I practise what I preach? How can I expect my children to live up to certain standards if I don't live up to them myself?

One of the most valuable lessons I think I can teach my children is the value of failure. We all fail at times, but as long as we learn from these experiences, they are not wasted.

I also know how important it is that my children know that I love them regardless of what they achieve, and whether or not they succeed. Obviously I want them to work hard and do their best, and I encourage them to do so at every opportunity, but I don't want them to grow up feeling that they will only be loved if they achieve high grades, have high-flying jobs and earn lots of money. To me, life is about so much more than this.

Our children are subject to tremendous peer pressure to own the latest mobile phone, games console or other gadget. I want my children to grow up knowing that these things are less important than who we are inside. I am trying to instil in them godly values and the importance of honesty, respect and consideration for other people. Perhaps this is countercultural, but I believe they need to learn that, without these values, the relationships they have in their lives will not be as fulfilling as they otherwise could be.

I am trying to teach my children that people and relationships are more important than money and status. As they grow older, I would much rather they earn less money doing a job they love, and feel fulfilled as they do it, than earn a fortune doing a job they detest, dreading Monday morning coming round each week. Of course, I encourage them to work hard at their studies so that they will have more opportunities open to them, but I want them to understand that true contentment doesn't come from money or possessions.

If we are constantly striving after the next new gadget, or a bigger house, or a better car, I believe we can never be happy. There will always be something more, something bigger, to own or strive for, no matter how much we already have. The Apostle Paul in the Bible says that he has 'learned the secret of being content in any and every situation',[1] and I believe we should try to cultivate the attitude of being grateful for what we have, rather than always wanting more.

I believe that the most important thing I can encourage my children to have is a relationship with Jesus. If they know Him and follow Him through their lives, they won't go far wrong. I know they will face their fair share of struggles, as we all do, but I also know that if they lean on him, He will enable them to cope, just as He always has helped me through the difficult times in my life.

---

[1] Philippians 4:12.

Chapter 4
'Moses? It's God calling...'

Something I find really helpful when I am reading, particularly when I'm reading the Bible, is to try to put myself in the shoes of the person I am reading about. I think we can learn so much by trying to think about what the person would have been feeling, why they acted in the way they did, what their motivation was, and so on.

The Bible is full of colourful characters, and I think we can learn so much from them, whatever our background and beliefs.

Ordinary, or extraordinary?

All through the Bible we read about people whom God called to do a job who didn't feel that they were up to the task. Moses, for example, didn't feel able to speak, Jeremiah and Solomon said they were too young, Gideon thought he was too small and insignificant.[2] But God used all of these people, and many, many more, to fulfil His plans. And He still does it today. He takes ordinary people and does extraordinary things through them.

Let's think about Mother Teresa. She was just an ordinary woman who was motivated by her compassion for the poor. In 1950 she founded the Missionaries of Charity, an organisation that exists to work with and for the poorest of the poor

---

[2] See Exodus 3–4; Jeremiah 1:6-7; 1 Kings 3:7; Judges 6:15-40.

throughout the world. Through Mother Teresa and this organisation, God has transformed the lives of many people, and not just the poor with whom they work. Many westerners have been inspired by Mother Teresa's example and have gone on to make a real difference in their own communities. If Anjezë Gonxhe Bojaxhiu had considered that she was too ordinary to make a difference, what a loss that would have been for the world.

Mother Teresa was a very humble woman, yet she didn't consider that she wasn't good enough to make a difference. She saw need, and knew that it was within her capability to do something about it, even if what she did made just a small difference.

She didn't allow fame and recognition to change her either; she stayed true to herself, and followed the plan that God had mapped out for her. And God used her to make a big difference, probably much bigger than she had ever hoped or dreamed.

Sorry, God, I can't do it

One of the best-known characters in the Bible is Moses. He brought the Israelites out of slavery in Egypt and led them as they wandered in the wilderness for 40 years. He had a very close relationship with God – his face would shine so much after he had been in God's presence that he had to wear a veil, and he was the only one who was permitted to enter God's presence and speak with Him.

But it wasn't always that way. When God first called Moses and told him of the job He wanted him to do, which was to confront Pharaoh and tell him to set the Israelites free, Moses protested. Five times he told God that he didn't feel capable, and would God please send somebody else![3]

Does that sound familiar? How often do we think that we're not capable, that we're not up to the job? This is certainly something I can relate to. But I believe God will always give us the tools and the abilities we need to do what we are called to do, just as He equipped Moses, even though we may be challenged and taken out of our comfort zone at times. Sometimes the hardest person to convince of our own ability is ourselves.

I don't know why Moses didn't feel up to the task he was being asked to undertake. Perhaps his confidence and self-esteem were low. He had committed murder 40 years previously and had run away, so he probably thought he would be the last person that God would want to use. Consider what he said to God: 'Who am I that I should go to Pharaoh and bring the Israelites out of Egypt?'[4] In effect he was saying, 'I can't do it; I'm not good enough.'

God refused to take no for an answer. He was very patient, and answered Moses' hesitations, telling him what to say and showing him how to deal with the obstacles he might encounter. But Moses still resisted.

In the end, though, God began to get frustrated with Moses, and at that point Moses gave in. Perhaps he finally realised he wasn't going to win against God, or maybe he was finally convinced by what God said to him and the signs He gave him.

The point is that when God gave Moses a job to do, He made sure He gave him the skills and resources he needed to do it – He told him what to say, He gave him signs to perform in front of Pharaoh, He gave him Aaron as a spokesman, and He gave Moses the courage, even if Moses didn't recognise these things initially.

---

[3] See Exodus 3:11, 13; 4;1, 10, 13.
[4] Exodus 3:11.

I believe that this is the same for us. We may be asked to do something that we don't feel capable of doing, but if it is God who is asking us to do it, I believe He will equip us.

Sometimes it's not until we step out in faith and start to do whatever it is that we realise that we actually *are* capable of doing it. I can think of a number of times when I haven't felt that I would be capable of doing a particular thing, but I have found that, as I have attempted to do it, I have surprised myself and realised that actually I was able to.

A speaker I was listening to recently gave a great analogy for this. He likened it to walking through automatic doors. If we wait for the doors to open before we walk towards them, we will wait for ever and they will never open. The doors will only open as we walk towards them. As we step out in faith, believing that the doors will open, they will, and then we will be able to walk through them.

We do need to be discerning, though, because if we try to do something that isn't within our calling, we may well find we don't have the necessary capabilities and may find we fall flat on our faces. But even if we do, God is kind and gracious, and will always pick us up again, dust us down, and set us back on the right path.

When I feel challenged about something I need to do, I find it helpful sometimes to try to pinpoint exactly what it is that I am afraid of. Why don't I feel capable of doing this particular thing? Is it because I genuinely don't think I have the ability, or am I just afraid of other people's reactions? Is this the unrealistic perfectionist in me worrying about making a mistake? Am I being oversensitive?

If I can narrow it down to one or two particular things that I can then deal with head on, I find it much easier to manage the whole problem.

I also find it helpful to approach the situation one step at a time. If I'm feeling a little overwhelmed before I begin a big work project, or I need to get started on a difficult assignment for my course, I think about the first step that I need to take and then move forward from there. Invariably I find that subsequent steps become easier as I go along. Looking at the task in its entirety can freeze me into inactivity, but taking it step by step breaks it down into manageable chunks.

Looking up to the top of the mountain can leave us thinking we'll never get there – it's just way too high – but if we focus on getting past one ledge at a time, we'll reach the summit in the end. And how good does it feel to look down from the top and see how far we've come, to look back at what we've managed to achieve? The view from the top is great, isn't it?!

Moses was obedient, even though he felt inadequate. This (initially) timid man, lacking in confidence and self-belief, is considered to be one of the greatest leaders in history.

Taking a risk

God initially gave Moses two tasks. First he was to go to the Israelite leaders and convince them that God had sent him and Aaron to liberate the people; then he was to go to Pharaoh and tell him to set the Israelites free.

The Israelite leaders believed Moses and Aaron immediately.[5] I like to think that this was all part of God's plan. When Moses and Aaron were successful in carrying out the first instruction and the Israelite leaders believed them, this would have given them more confidence to go ahead and carry out the second, much bigger task. Small victories inspire us to go on and fight bigger battles.

God did warn Moses in advance that the second task wouldn't be an easy battle, and that Pharaoh's heart would be

---

[5] Exodus 4:29-31.

hardened, but I doubt whether Moses was expecting it to be as tough as it was.

As predicted, Pharaoh said 'No' to Moses, that he wouldn't let the Israelites go. But not only did he say 'No', he also made things much worse for the Israelites. He instructed them to produce the same number of bricks each day, but they would no longer be supplied with straw – they would now have to go and find their own straw. As a result, the Israelites stopped believing Moses and blamed him for these harsh conditions.

So, understandably, the Israelites were angry, and they complained to Moses and Aaron. Moses and Aaron must have been quite confused by everything that was going on. I wonder whether Moses' new-found confidence would have taken a bit of a beating at this point. Perhaps he began to doubt himself, even though God had warned him it would be difficult. Maybe he thought, 'Did I hear God right? Did I get it wrong? Was it something I said to Pharaoh that ruined God's plan? Was it my fault?'

When God told him to go back to Pharaoh again and tell him to set the people free, Moses protested again. To be honest, I don't really blame him. After things had gone so well initially with the Israelite leaders, now they had gone horribly wrong; instead of things getting better they had only got worse. It's not really surprising that Moses was reluctant to do or say anything more.[6] Moses questioned God, saying:

> Why, Lord, why have you brought trouble on this people? Is this why you sent me? Ever since I went to Pharaoh to speak in your name, he has brought trouble on this people, and you have not rescued your people at all.
> *Exodus 5:22-23*

---

[6] Exodus 6:12.

It is easy for us now to understand what was going on – we have the benefit of being able to see the whole picture, and we know that God did have a plan – but for Moses, who had no idea what the future held, it must have been very confusing, and I'm sure he wondered what on earth God was doing. God had promised liberation, but instead of improving, things were getting steadily worse.

Moses had serious doubts, but God was gentle and persistent. He spoke again to Moses and reassured him that he had heard him correctly, and Moses somehow summoned up the courage to go and speak to Pharaoh again. Not just once more, but *nine times* more. Several times his hopes were lifted – Pharaoh said yes, he would let the people go – and every time they were dashed again when Pharaoh changed his mind.

Each time Pharaoh said no to Moses, God sent a plague on Egypt – blood, frogs, gnats, flies, death of livestock, boils, hail, locusts and darkness. Each of these plagues made reference to one of the Egyptian gods, and through them God showed that He was in ultimate control. Pharaoh's advisers were unable to control these plagues, and in this way God highlighted the impotence of the Egyptian gods.

However, despite the displays of God's unmatchable power, Pharaoh would not change his mind and he refused to let the people go. Until the last time, when God sent the tenth, most serious, plague. Pharaoh finally realised that God meant business, and took Him seriously. He realised that he could never win against God, and he agreed to let the Israelites go. But even then he changed his mind again, and sent his army after them. But God continued to be faithful to the Israelites. He defeated the Egyptian army by miraculously enabling the Israelites to pass through the Red Sea on dry land.[7]

All through this roller coaster of a journey, through all its ups and downs, every time their hopes were raised and dashed

---

[7] Exodus 14:5-31.

again, God was with Moses and Aaron. How many times must they have felt like giving up, that the plan would never work, that Pharaoh would never give in? But in spite of the opposition and the hardship, they persisted and continued to do what God had told them to.

It must have been very hard, and they must have felt very isolated. Even the very people they were fighting for had turned against them. Yet they persevered. They believed in what they had to do and they carried on, even though it looked as though the odds were severely stacked against them.

As I look back over my own life, there have been times when I didn't have a clue what was going on and I really didn't know how things were going to turn out. But as I look back now, with the benefit of hindsight, I can see that there was a plan in place, and that by sticking with what I thought was the right thing to do at the time, things did work out. I cling to this at difficult times even now, and I know that God is in control, even if I can't see through the fog and know how it's going to turn out in the end.

I have learnt a lot from Moses' story, and I know there is still so much that I can glean from it. The confidence to have the courage of my convictions is an important lesson I'm learning, especially if others don't agree with me. I may be wrong, and if I am I will admit it and deal with the consequences. On the other hand, I may be right, and I may open up new and exciting avenues to explore and enjoy.

I'm not naturally a risk taker and I always weigh up the pros and cons before I make any decisions, and I always pray to God for guidance, but I'm learning to take calculated risks, and knowing that God is on my side is very reassuring. I might fall now and again, and I might get it wrong sometimes, but I will be able to pick myself up again and move on. My pride might take a bit of a battering, but that won't do me any harm.

Chapter 5
Reaching out

Likewise, the tongue is a small part of the body, but it
makes great boasts. Consider what a great forest is set
on fire by a small spark.
James 3:5

The power of words

I have always been aware that the way we communicate can
build or destroy relationships. When I was a teenager, a
passing remark that someone made about something that was
dear to my heart cut me deeply, and I felt that the rug had been
pulled out from under me. For someone whose confidence was
already low, this was very damaging. The fact that I remember
it so clearly to this day shows that it had a profound effect on
me.

I realised then that words have great power, and I
determined that I would always do my best not to hurt others
with my words. I resolved to think before I spoke about how
my words might impact others, how they might make the other
person feel, how they would make me feel if they were said to
me. Perhaps this is partly why I became so tongue-tied – I was
so afraid that what I said might be misinterpreted or cause
offence that I thought it would be better to say nothing at all;
that, and the fact that I didn't feel I had anything interesting to
say. But it meant that my relationships suffered greatly.

Words can be extremely powerful. Words can harm or they
can heal. Words can divide or they can unite. Words can
destroy or they can build up. We need to think very carefully

about how we use our words in order that their effect is constructive, not destructive. When words are used destructively, those on the receiving end can be left feeling undermined, undervalued, unloved or, at worst, completely worthless.

As I mentioned earlier, part of my journey into self-acceptance meant that I began to understand that not everything that went wrong around me was my fault. This was a very important step for me. It meant that I was able to observe more objectively what was happening in my relationships and the way other people communicated with and related to me. Very slowly, I began to be able to recognise unhealthy communication behaviours in others.

It was very difficult to learn to stand up for myself, but gradually I was able to identify when others were putting me down with their words. I had always just accepted this before, as I considered that what they said must be true, but now that I had begun to be able to see a little more objectively, somehow I started to find the courage to challenge these statements. Beginning to love myself for who I was, and am, enabled me to understand that others should love me for who I am too, and if they didn't, then there was something wrong – and perhaps the fault wasn't only with me.

As we learn to love and accept ourselves, the way we relate to other people changes. I have noticed that I am now much more open with people and I am not afraid to be myself any more, even with people I don't know. I feel much more relaxed with people, and I think people therefore feel more relaxed with me.

As I look at the close relationships I have, it is fairly obvious that I relate much more easily to people with whom I have things in common – perhaps they have similar interests, or are at a similar life stage to me. I tend to get on well with people of a similar personality type to me, because we seem to understand each other, although I also gravitate towards some people who are very different to me. I notice that extroverts sometimes bring me out of myself, and if I'm with talkative people I sometimes become more talkative as well.

There are particular personality traits that I warm to immediately – honesty and openness, genuine humility and modesty, a sense of humour that is similar to my own, shared beliefs and values, and so on. At times, though, I just can't put my finger on what it is about a person that I take to. I realise that I will automatically get on better with some people than with others, and I am now able to accept that this is just how things are and that it is not a personal rejection of me, or of the other person.

It's not what we say, it's the way we say it

A vital element of every relationship we have is communication. Without good communication, there can be no relationship. And when communication breaks down, a relationship cannot survive.

Communication is about so much more than the words we speak: it is said that when we communicate face to face, a large percentage of what we say is conveyed non-verbally, perhaps even more than 90%. Tone of voice is said to account for around 38% of what we 'say', and other non-verbal signals for around 55%. This leaves just 7% for our words to have impact.[8] It's not much, is it? The words we say are important, but just as important, or perhaps even more so, is the way we say them.

As I look back on my life, I wonder what kind of non-verbal signals I was giving off when my self-esteem was very low.

---

[8] This is a fairly well-known theory. See, for example, Judi James (2008), *The Body Language Bible*, Vermilion, p.11.

Obviously I don't remember, as I wasn't aware of it at the time, but I am pretty sure that I would have been giving out negative signals. Because I was so shy, my stance was probably automatically 'closed', giving the impression that I didn't want to let people in. Perhaps I would fold my arms, or turn away slightly from the person I was talking to. I'm pretty sure I would have struggled to make eye contact. I didn't intentionally shut people out, but it must have been very difficult to have a conversation with me when I was giving the impression that I wasn't interested.

As I began to realise these things, I made a conscious effort to appear to be more relaxed and more confident, even if I didn't feel it on the inside. It was something I had had to do at various times during my life anyway, on occasions such as job interviews, but I found it so difficult, and so draining! On these occasions, I just kept thinking about the objective – I really wanted the job and I knew what I had to do to get it – but the necessary behaviour didn't come naturally to me; I really had to work at it.

Now I had a different objective – I wanted to form real relationships – and I knew I would have to dig deep to do what needed to be done in order to achieve this objective. Describing it in this way makes it sound quite impersonal and calculated, but that's not how it was. I just knew that if I really wanted these relationships, I would have to work hard to make it happen. Gradually it became easier, and certainly, as the relationships began to grow, I began to feel more comfortable with people and began to be able to relax.

Meeting new people is still something I find quite difficult, but I am learning to manage this situation too, and it is becoming easier as time goes on. I remind myself that I am a normal, likeable person; I tell myself that there is no reason that they will not accept or like me for who I am; I take a deep breath and make a conscious effort to smile and look relaxed. I still worry that I will say something to make myself look silly, but, in fact, this happens much less often than I think it will. And if it does, I try not to take it to heart, tell myself we all do it, perhaps laugh about it, and move on with the rest of the conversation.

Every relationship is a risk. We might get hurt, it might not work out, or we might hurt the other person. This does happen sometimes, but if we hide away out of fear, we will lose out on so much. It hurts like mad when relationships go wrong, but I believe that what we will gain from good relationships is worth the risk. At those times when it does go wrong, we can lean on the other relationships that we have in order to carry us through. Yes, it's extremely painful, but in time the pain does lessen.

As I look back and see how my life and relationships have unfolded, I am convinced that God made sure that I had these relationships in place for many reasons. Obviously relationships are important for all of us because we are created to be relational beings, and God was filling a big gap in my life. But I also believe He made sure I had these growing friendships because He knew what was around the corner. He made sure that I had what I needed to get through what was going to be a particularly difficult time in my life. He had gently but firmly guided me into the friendships I was now able to enjoy in order that I would be able to lean on my friends when I needed them most.

Chapter 6
When relationships break down

Be strong and courageous. Do not be afraid; do not be
discouraged, for the Lord your God will be with you
wherever you go.
Joshua 1:9

A number of years ago I went through a marriage break-up and
divorce. It was, needless to say, a very difficult time. It was
something that I never thought would happen to me. I believe
marriage is for life, and it wasn't something that I entered into
lightly. I believed at the time that it was the right thing, and I
was fully committed to the marriage.

Then things started to go wrong. If I'm honest, the marriage
died a long time before we actually separated, but I didn't
consider divorce to be an option for me. So I attempted to paper
over the cracks (which were more like gaping holes, to be
honest) and stuck with it because I thought it was the best thing
for the children, and I'd made my bed and now had to lie in it,
so to speak. I made the best of it and did everything I could to
build a happy life for the family.

However, things eventually got to the point where they
were becoming damaging for all concerned, particularly the
children. As soon as I realised that the children would suffer
more if I stayed in the marriage than if I left, I took steps to
separate. I still wrestled with the whole issue of divorce,
though, but God was gracious. He spoke to me clearly, saying
that He would be with me along whatever path I chose to
follow.

Deep inside I knew that this was the confirmation I had been
hoping for. I knew that God was saying that I'd struggled on

for long enough and that I could be released from this relationship. So I filed for divorce.

Knowing that God was with me made it a lot easier, but it was still desperately hard. I was emotionally battered and bruised, but somehow I managed to pick up the pieces and carry on.

The hardest thing was seeing how much it hurt the children. My daughter was quite young and much of what had been going on fortunately went over her head, but the boys were a little older and both very sensitive to what was going on around them. It broke my heart to see the pain they were both going through. I felt helpless, but I had my faith, my friends and my family around me to see us through.

Acknowledging our feelings

At times I felt that all I could do was to pray. I prayed so hard for the children, and I gave them every opportunity to talk to me about how they felt. But I knew they would find it difficult to be really honest with me about their feelings, particularly if they were angry with me for asking their dad to leave, so I made sure they had opportunities to talk to other people who would listen to them and help them through.

These were people who they knew would be objective, who wouldn't judge them, and who would just listen to what they had to say. It was so important for them to know they could shout and scream at someone if they wanted to, or just talk through how they were feeling without being criticised for how they felt. They didn't always take up the opportunities, but I think it helped a lot knowing that people were there if they needed them.

I remember saying to the children at the time how important it was for them to acknowledge how they were feeling. I believe that how we feel is never wrong, and it is so important to acknowledge the way we feel. We may be angry, or sad, or frustrated, and it is important that we understand not only how we feel but why we feel that way.

What we do with our feelings, though, is important: the way we react or respond can be right or wrong, and we must be careful that we don't lash out in anger or frustration. This is why it is so important to talk through our feelings; talking things through with someone who will listen patiently, without judging, is vitally important.

Picking up the pieces

As I look back, I can honestly say that God has done an amazing work of healing in all of us. I'm not saying the experience hasn't left scars, but the pain has gone, and we are restored.

My eldest son found the whole time particularly hard, and withdrew into himself for months. But as I and many others continued to pray, God reached in and pulled him free.

I remember a particularly significant shopping trip which told me how far he had come. For months he had only worn black and grey t-shirts, which to me symbolised how he was feeling on the inside. On this particular occasion he picked up three t-shirts he wanted me to buy for him. One was green, one was blue, the other was orange – all bright colours! I must have had the biggest smile on my face as I paid for them, and it was such a joy to see him wear them!

One of the most important things I learned through all of this was to give the children time and space to process everything that had happened. Obviously I needed time and space to work it all through as well, but to be honest, I had done all my grieving for the marriage over the previous years, and I just felt relieved to be free.

Please understand me here. I am not saying that the solution for every difficult marriage is to separate and start again. I still believe that marriage is for life, and I sincerely wish that none of us had had to go through the pain that we did.

If you are in the same situation, I would urge you to do everything you can to save your marriage. Don't throw away all the years you have invested in the relationship if there is a chance it can be saved. If both parties are willing, counselling can help enormously; relationships *can* be saved, even if they appear to be hopeless. Even if you think there is no hope for your marriage, I would encourage you to seek counselling. It will help you to see things from a different perspective, and hopefully it will give you some clarity for the future.

If there is even the slightest glimmer of hope, I believe that a relationship should be worked at, that the years of investment shouldn't be thrown away lightly. In my situation I knew that things would never improve, and a marriage counselling session confirmed very clearly that there was no way back. I knew that this was the only way forward for me and the children. It wasn't an easy option, but it was the right one for us.

Forgiveness

One of the hardest things I had to do was to forgive, yet I knew that Jesus placed great importance on forgiveness. I have always found His teaching on this subject very challenging. When Peter asked Him how many times we should forgive when we are wronged, Jesus said 'seventy-seven times'.[9] This is a symbolic number that, in fact, means an infinite amount of times.

I realised that if I didn't forgive, and if I held on to my anger and resentment, I would end up damaging myself and the children. It wouldn't make the slightest difference to the person I was angry with whether I forgave or not! Believe me, it would have been very easy for me to let it fester and allow it to eat me up inside, but I knew that if I did that, I would end up being very unhappy.

I also realised that to forgive would take away any power that the person concerned might have over me. If I were to forgive and move on, the past would no longer have any effect on me and I would be free.

In so many situations I think we find it so much easier to wallow in our hurt and dwell on how we have been wounded. Our sense of justice has been wronged. 'It's just not fair.' But this isn't what Jesus tells us to do, and with good reason. He knows what damage unforgiveness can do to us.

Jesus also tells us that we will be judged by the same measure that we use to judge others:

> For in the same way as you judge others, you will be judged, and with the measure you use, it will be measured to you.
> *Matthew 7:2*

It was one of the hardest things I have ever done, but bit by bit I managed to let it go.

I wouldn't be honest if I said things from the past didn't come back to haunt me occasionally; they still do, but when that happens I try to recognise it for what it is and think about

---

[9] Matthew 18:21-22.

what it will do to me if I don't let it go. As time goes on it becomes easier to let go and to control the effect it has on me.

Having people around me who can see when this is happening is a big help. Sometimes I fall back into old habits and patterns of behaviour, into automatic responses to situations or things people say or do, and these people enable me to take a step back and see things more objectively.

I believe we are able to choose how we respond to situations, and we must be aware of the difference between responding and reacting. A reaction is something that is instinctive, something we do automatically without thinking about it; we don't always have control over our reactions. A response, on the other hand, is something that we think about before we do it; it is measured and thought through. We control it; it doesn't control us.

When I say we are able to choose how we respond to a situation, I am talking about two types of response. I mean that we are able to have control both over how we respond at the time to the other person, and over how we will allow it to affect us.

I have had conversations with a number of people who had very difficult childhoods and I have observed how some appear to have found it extremely difficult to let go of the anger and resentment they feel about some of the things that happened to them. Others, on the other hand, have tried to learn from their experiences and appear to have resolved not to make the same mistakes in their own lives. I have also noticed that the latter ones – those who have tried to learn from their experiences and use them in a positive way – seem to be more balanced and happier people.

Choices

From my observations and experiences, I realise that I have a choice with every experience I go through, particularly the difficult ones. As time goes on, I try to look at each situation with objective eyes and to think about the choices I have. I try to look into each alternative and think about what the consequences might be of the responses I might choose.

If, for example, I had allowed my hurt and anger from my difficult marriage to take over, what might the results of that have been? I think it would have eaten away at me inside; it would have hindered any chance I might have had of a relationship in the future (not that I was looking for one!); it might have damaged my ability to trust people at all, and my bitterness would have had an adverse effect on the children. Having learnt to trust people and let them in, I didn't want to lose what I had found. Learning to trust people had also taught me that not everybody is untrustworthy – I just needed to choose wisely who to put my trust in.

I knew that holding on to the resentment and anger would only have damaged me as a person. So instead of allowing it to eat away at me, I chose to look for learning opportunities in the experience. I talked through how I was feeling with close friends. Just talking about things helped me to see them from a different perspective and helped me to deal with my feelings and emotions. I was aware as I talked that sometimes I went over the same ground several times, but each time was a necessary part of the healing process.

I also learnt the difference between forgiveness and reconciliation. They are not the same thing. It is important to forgive, but if a relationship is damaging, it might not be appropriate to be reconciled with that person. In such a situation, and if there is no hope of improvement, putting ourselves or others (such as our children) back into the same setting is not to be advised.

I am also learning to forgive myself. Not forgiving ourselves can eat away at us inside just as much as not forgiving another person. This is always something I have found very difficult, as I alluded to in an earlier chapter. I have always been very hard on myself and find it very difficult to forgive myself for my shortcomings. But I know this is a vital step on my journey. We must learn to forgive ourselves when we make mistakes.

Our mistakes may have consequences for other people. This can be very hard to deal with. Our conscience will prick us, or even stab us repeatedly, when we think about things that we have done and the way they have affected other people's lives. I am learning, though, that in the same way I need to take responsibility for my own responses to situations, other people need to take responsibility for their responses too. I am not saying we can absolve ourselves of all responsibility – indeed, it is important to do everything we can to make things right – but sometimes there is only so much we can do.

What I find enormously helpful in situations like these is to pray. I believe that God is a God of miracles, and that He can put right what I can't. I have seen this in my own children. One of my biggest fears was that they would be permanently damaged and scarred by my marriage break-up, but as you have read, God has worked a miracle. As I said, there are still scars, but my ongoing prayer is that they will examine their experiences for themselves and seek to learn from them.

I have never tried to hide what I went through. I am not ashamed of it, but I am not proud of it either. It is something that happened to me and it is one of the many things that have shaped the person I am today.

One of the interesting things I have noticed since all this happened is that people who are going through, or have been through, similar events will much more readily open up and discuss their experiences with me. This is a real privilege, and I find it truly humbling. I think people are more comfortable talking about sensitive and personal issues with someone who they feel understands how hard it is, and the pain that is involved.

Chapter 7
The importance of honesty and trust

The Lord detests lying lips, but he delights in people
who are trustworthy.
Proverbs 12:22

I believe that a relationship without trust is only a shell. Without trust, there can be little depth to a relationship. The trust had broken down in my marriage, but I was fortunate enough at the time to have a number of close friends and family members whom I did trust. They were there for me when I needed them, and they didn't let me down.

This helped me to realise that I could still trust people and enabled me to understand that, just because the trust had broken down in one relationship, it didn't mean that it would automatically break down in every relationship I had. Equally though, I wasn't about to bare my soul to everyone I met; I am a naturally cautious person anyway, and my experiences reinforced this tendency within me.

After my marriage break-up, I was very happy to be on my own with the children, and thought I was going to be single for the rest of my life. I needed to be there for the children, and with three of them to look after, two part-time jobs and a house to run, I figured that there was no way I would have time for a relationship, even if I wanted one!

Isn't it amazing how life never works out how we imagine it to? As I say, my intention was to remain single, and I was very happy with that thought. I didn't need anyone; indeed, I didn't want to get involved with anyone. It would have been far too complicated, it wouldn't have been fair on the children, and I didn't have the time. But God had other ideas...

God is full of surprises!

A little under a year later, I met Pete. He had been coming along to the church for a while, and one evening we got chatting. After a few weeks I had a feeling he was beginning to like me as more than just a friend, and I panicked! I didn't know what to do. I prayed about it, and I chatted with a couple of friends about it. Once they stopped laughing (in the nicest possible way), they prayed for me too!

A couple of weeks later Pete asked me if I would like to go for lunch with him. I said yes, and we arranged to meet the following weekend.

I spent the whole week worrying about it. I didn't know if I was being fair to Pete, as I didn't know whether I could ever get involved with anyone again, let alone so soon. I was 'damaged goods', and I didn't know how much I had in me to give. But God spoke to me clearly through a book I was reading at the time, and made it clear that it would all be okay and that I should trust Him on this.

I was still very nervous about the relationship, and my fears were still there – what if it doesn't work out? What if I get hurt? What if I hurt him? How will it affect the children? Is this fair to the children after what they have been through?

But I knew God was telling me to trust Him, and I knew I could trust God. He had never let me down before, and I knew He never would. So I put my hand in God's hand and said I would walk the road with Him, but could we please take it slowly?!

Saturday came around, and Pete and I met in a coffee shop before going for lunch. I'd been thinking all week about what I was going to say to him, as I knew I needed to be honest with him right from the start about where I was coming from and about how I wasn't sure what I was capable of giving to a relationship.

In my head I'd prepared a speech, and the words all came tumbling out as soon as we sat down. I told Pete about my marriage break-up, that I was fragile and hurt, that I didn't know whether I could get involved with anyone again, and that I didn't want to risk hurting him by getting involved and then perhaps not being able to give him what he wanted. I said I wanted to be friends (with hugs – he gives such good hugs) and was that okay with him.

I think Pete was quite shocked by my frankness! But I know he appreciated my honesty, and he was very happy to take things at a pace I felt I could cope with.

God was able to continue His work of healing in me through Pete. God had done so much already, over the previous year, but there was still much unfinished business, even though I didn't realise it at the time. Looking back, I don't think these issues could ever have been dealt with without my getting involved with someone again. I had to learn to trust Pete, to let him in, and to take a risk. Although I had friends I trusted, this was different. It was very hard to allow someone to get so close, but God knew what He was doing.

Pete was very patient and didn't put pressure on me to move things along any faster than I was comfortable with, which was exactly what I needed. He was (and still is) very perceptive about my feelings, and somehow seems to know how I am feeling without my having to tell him.

This was actually quite scary to begin with. We had known each other for about three weeks when he picked up from a text message that I wasn't feeling myself. I still don't know how he did it, and to be honest it frightened me that he knew me so well already! Had I really given so much of myself away?! How could I have let my guard down? For someone who was used to keeping my feelings firmly to myself, and to being firmly in control, this was really quite difficult to cope with.

Now I have got used to being known so well, it is actually very refreshing and reassuring. Just to know that someone understands exactly how I feel, without my having to explain it to them, is very liberating. To be able to acknowledge how I feel without having to explain and justify myself is very affirming.

This has given me increased confidence to be who I am with other people too, and to say what I think about things. For many years I felt that I had to explain myself, to justify myself and how I felt, and almost that I had to apologise for my opinion. I wouldn't have the confidence to offer my point of view in a discussion, and I would do absolutely everything I could to avoid confrontation. But I'm learning that, actually, my opinion *is* valid. I do have a right to a say, and it is quite acceptable to disagree with what someone else thinks. I will even initiate such a discussion at times, if I feel it is necessary to clear the air, rather than trying to brush an issue under the carpet and pretend it doesn't exist.

One of the other things that helped to build my confidence further was the honesty Pete showed towards me. Over many years I had become used to being lied to, and to having secrets kept from me. When Pete and I first went out he was very open and honest about himself. This was not only very refreshing, but it made me feel valued. The fact that he respected me enough to be truthful with me, and thought I was important enough to be open about himself with me, really meant a lot to me.

Building blocks

It takes time to build trust, and there are a number of things that help us decide whether or not to trust someone. Some of this is instinctive – we sometimes just 'feel' that we can trust someone – but our instincts can, sadly, let us down at times.

Observing the other relationships people have can be an indicator of whether or not someone is trustworthy. If they are clearly trusted by other people, that is a good sign. If other people appear to be wary of the person, perhaps that is a warning signal that we ought to be cautious too.

Time is another important element in building trust. Over time, we build up a track record with people, and they build up one with us. During this time we are able to observe whether a person is consistent – whether their words are backed up by their actions. It is said that actions speak louder than words, and to me this is so true. Words are easy to say; actions take more effort. Words that are not backed up by actions are meaningless.

You might be able to guess that one of my love languages is 'acts of service'. One way I know and trust that Pete loves me is because his actions support his words. It is easy for him to tell me he loves me, but when he gets out of bed to make me a cup of tea in the mornings, or gets up from the armchair just to warm up my microwaveable slippers because my feet are cold, I know he loves me because these things take much more effort. I know I can trust his love for me because his actions back up his words. (Incidentally, I highly recommend microwaveable slippers if you suffer with cold feet – they are fantastic!)

Another sign of whether a person is trustworthy is whether they are true to their word. Do they make promises they don't keep, or do they make every effort to follow through when they have given their word? We soon learn whether or not we can trust someone to do what they say they are going to do. Following through on our promises is very important.

It's funny, isn't it, how at times, words can be meaningless, yet at other times they have a tremendous impact on us? It seems to me that the relationship we have with a person has a direct bearing on the impact their words have on us. If they are someone close to us, their words have a great effect on us. If we trust the person, their words mean everything, and we rely on them without question. If the person is someone more distant from us, or if we don't feel able to trust them, their words can bounce off us without having any effect at all.

I also find it interesting to note that we react far more to negative words than to positive words. Ten positive things might be said about us or to us, and one negative thing. Why is it that we choose to focus on the one negative thing? Perhaps this goes back to our inherent need to be loved and accepted, and negative words can feel like a form of rejection.

Can I encourage you to embrace the positive things that people say about you? Don't filter them out in favour of the negative things. Keep them all in perspective.

Chapter 8
The ongoing journey

'For I know the plans I have for you,' declares the
Lord, 'plans to prosper you and not to harm you,
plans to give you hope and a future.'
Jeremiah 29:11

To finish the story, or rather this chapter of it, Pete and I were
married a year after our first date. Our relationship moved
forward pretty quickly in the end! Our wedding was such a
wonderful day, and it was a real joy to celebrate with our
family, our friends and our church family. Every person there
was special to us, and there were some who sadly were unable
to join us, but to celebrate with many of the people who were
journeying with us, loving us, supporting us and rooting for us,
was so moving.

When I look back at the person I was and the person I am
now, I can see how far I have come. Many people and
experiences have made me who I am today, and I know that
my ongoing experiences and relationships will continue to
shape me. I realise how blessed I am and have been to have
good friends and family around me to love me, encourage me
and support me.

Having come through some of the things I have been
through, I realise just how blessed I am. I try not to take
anything for granted, and I really value what I have. Even little
things to me are special – a kind word, a thoughtful deed. Even
things like having a cup of tea or a meal made for me are
appreciated, as I know these actions are expressions of love.

Some people say that they would love to be 21 again. I
understand what they mean, but I wouldn't – not unless I could

have the knowledge and experience that I have now! I wouldn't want to go back again to having little confidence, low self-esteem and feeling unworthy of being loved.

As I move from feeling 'less than ordinary' to enjoying the extraordinary things that are unfolding in my life, I am looking forward to seeing what else lies in store. I know the path won't always be smooth, but I trust that God will see me through the darker times, as He always has so far.

In addition to meeting Pete and getting married, my life has taken a number of other unexpected turns recently. I am now doing a number of things I never thought I would ever do: I left my part-time job in the church office to focus full-time on my freelance career, and I have begun studying a degree in Theology part-time. I have also written this book. None of these things was expected – they all came completely out of the blue. And I know without a doubt that each one is absolutely right for me at this point in my life.

A little while ago I watched a short film called *The Butterfly Circus*. I would strongly encourage you to watch it if you can – it's about 20 minutes long and is freely available on the internet.[10] It's a very moving film, a beautiful portrayal of how we are all different, and how we all have something special and unique to offer, no matter what our limitations are.

Less visible is not less important

Another important thing I am beginning to appreciate is that we don't need to have a highly visible role in order to play a crucial part. What goes on in the background is just as

---

[10] See http://thebutterflycircus.com/short-film/. Accessed 8 April 2013.

important as what goes on in the spotlight. Let's go back to the story of the Israelites in Egypt.

Moses was God's front man, and through him God led the Israelites out of Egypt, but many others had a vital role to play too. The footnote to Exodus 2:10 in the *NIV Study Bible* makes the point that all of Pharaoh's efforts to suppress the Israelites were thwarted by women.[11]

I was fascinated by this when I read it. The point I want to make is not the fact that they were women, but that they were all figures in the background, doing things that they probably considered were not particularly important in the great scheme of things. As we read the account, it's easy to overlook these characters and their contributions.

Pharaoh was feeling threatened by the growth of the Israelite nation while they were in Egypt; he thought they were becoming too numerous, so he forced them into slavery. They continued to increase in number, however, so he gave instructions to the midwives attending the Hebrew births to kill all the baby boys.

What a dreadful situation for these poor midwives to be in – it doesn't even bear thinking about. However, the midwives did not obey Pharaoh because they feared God even more than they feared Pharaoh. Yet they risked their lives, and probably the lives of their families too, by disobeying these instructions. They would more than likely have been living every day in fear, looking over their shoulders, terrified that they would be found out. But their loyalty to God and to their people was rewarded in the end.

Moses' mother and sister also had a crucial part to play. They hid Moses for three months after he was born so that the Egyptians wouldn't find him and kill him along with all the other baby boys who were being slaughtered. Once it became

---

[11] Note to Exodus 2:10, *NIV Study Bible* (Zondervan, 2008) p89.

too difficult to hide him, they put him in a basket and placed him in the River Nile.

I often wonder why they did that. What were they expecting to happen? Did they know that Pharaoh's daughter frequented that area, and were they hoping she would rescue him? Or was it just sheer desperation, perhaps the last resort, in the hope that somehow God would intervene and that their efforts wouldn't turn out to be in vain? Whatever their motivation, how hard it must have been to let their child go in that way.

When Pharaoh's daughter found him, Moses' sister Miriam offered to find a Hebrew woman to look after him until he was old enough to live with Pharaoh's daughter. Pharaoh's daughter agreed to this, and Moses was entrusted to the care of his own mother.

So Moses was able to live for a while longer with his family, and Pharaoh's daughter even paid them for looking after him![12] What a blessing for his mother and family! I'm sure it wouldn't even have crossed the mind of Moses' mother during this time that her son would become one of the greatest leaders in all of history; she was just doing what any mother would have done – trying to protect her son.

Pharaoh's own daughter was another who was used to bring about God's plan. When she found the baby in the river, her instinctive reaction was rescue and protection. If she had known what the future held, I wonder whether her actions would have taken a different turn.

In addition to all this, when the Israelites finally left Egypt, God said that the women were to ask their Egyptian neighbours for gold, silver and clothing, which meant that they left Egypt with blessing and abundance, and not in poverty.[13]

Without all of these people playing their vital roles, the Israelites would not have survived, let alone thrived, in Egypt

---

[12] Exodus 2:1-10.
[13] Exodus 3:22.

and beyond. Without the courage of the midwives, the Israelite nation would have died out. Without the bravery of Moses' family, Moses would not have survived and gone on to become the great leader that God had created him to be. When he confronted Pharaoh 80 years later, how ironic that a member of Pharaoh's own family had rescued Moses as a baby and preserved his life! And without Moses eventually taking his courage in his hands and doing what God told him to do, the Israelites would not have been set free.

I take great encouragement from this story. As an ordinary person, living an ordinary life and doing ordinary things, I know that God can use me and these ordinary things to make a difference in my small corner of the world.

Moses was 80 years of age when he was given the task of speaking to Pharaoh and leading the Israelites out of Egypt. We are never too old for God to have a job for us. Neither are we ever too young. Consider Jeremiah: while he was still young, God told Jeremiah that He had appointed him 'as a prophet to the nations.'

Jeremiah didn't understand this at all, and said to God, 'Alas, Sovereign Lord ... I do not know how to speak; I am too young.'

But God replied, 'Do not say, "I am too young." You must go to everyone I send you to and say whatever I command you. Do not be afraid of them, for I am with you and will rescue you.' God then reached out and touched Jeremiah's mouth, saying, 'I have put my words in your mouth.'[14]

Abraham was an old man when God told him to leave his home and to go to a land that God would show him.[15] He was 90 years of age when God promised that He would make him a father of nations, and 100 when his son Isaac was born.

When we look at characters in the Bible, we see that God often chooses the least likely candidates to do great things. In a

---

[14] Jeremiah 1:5–9.
[15] Genesis 12:1.

society where it was everything to be the eldest son, and where the youngest was deemed to be unimportant, God looked favourably on many of the youngest. King David – one of the greatest kings of all time – was the youngest of eight sons. Gideon was from the weakest tribe in Manasseh, and he described himself as the least in his family.[16]

Whatever age we are; whether we are retired, studying, employed or unemployed; whatever job we do; whatever our personality, we are of infinite value to God, and we can be used by Him. He has a plan for each of us, and whatever that plan is, He will equip us with whatever we need to see it through.

The bigger picture

One of the ways my husband and I like to unwind is to do jigsaw puzzles. We love seeing the big picture take shape as we fill in the pieces one by one. Sometimes we do what are called 'Wasjigs', where you aren't given a picture of the puzzle on the box, but just some clues as to what the final picture will be.

I think jigsaw puzzles are a great analogy for life. All the individual pieces of the jigsaw represent our life experiences, which come together to form the bigger picture. I think, though, that in life, each individual piece contains a complete picture in itself, as well as forming a small part of the whole. I believe that every one of our life experiences is important for its own sake, and is not only about the part it forms of the bigger picture.

Let us not undervalue the relatively minor experiences in favour of focusing only on the ultimate plan for our lives. I believe each part of the journey is a complete experience in

---

[16] 1 Samuel 16:10-11; Judges 6:15.

itself and has much to teach us. The plan for our lives is made up of lots of little plans, as well as a big, overall one.

At the moment I'm not sure what God's long-term plan is for me, but I do know that whatever it is, it will be rewarding and probably challenging, but very exciting!

My personality, life experiences, abilities and skills are all important in shaping the person I am, and am becoming, and each one is a part of God's big plan for my life. But I realise, too, that every step of the journey is equally important, and as I go along, I am trying to look for the value in every experience, thinking about what I can learn from it, what it has to teach me, and how I can use it to become a better person.

Chapter 9
Are some people more equal than others?

For we are God's handiwork, created in Christ Jesus to
do good works, which God prepared in advance for
us to do.
Ephesians 2:10

It didn't take long for 'All animals are equal' to become 'All animals are equal, but some animals are more equal than others' in George Orwell's *Animal Farm*. This has always struck a chord with me, perhaps because deep down I felt it to be true. In my head I knew that all human beings are equal, but on the inside I didn't feel that I was equal to everyone else. I felt inferior – far less than equal to those around me.

As a woman, perhaps I have had a tendency to conform to society's expectations and to consider that I should rightfully take 'second place' to the men around me. I have certainly been affected by the attitudes of many people around me who held the view, whether consciously or not, that women are less important than men and were put on the earth to support men as they go about the 'important business' of life.

For most of my working life, the jobs I have done have fallen into the category of 'support staff', which hasn't helped, particularly as all the similar roles within the organisations I worked in were filled by women too.

It has taken a long time for me to appreciate my worth, not just as a human being, but as a woman.

I want to share some thoughts that have helped me to understand that I am of equal worth to God as every other human being who has ever walked the earth – both male and female.

As I write, Pete and I have been married for two and a half years. I still wrestle with the fact that he does his fair share, probably more, of the household chores. As a woman, I feel it is my obligation and my responsibility to do the washing, the cleaning, the cooking, etc, and I feel guilty when he does these things. We have an arrangement whereby I cook during the week, and Pete cooks at the weekends in order to free up my time to work, and he does much of the housework for the same reason.

Why do I feel guilty about this? I have a busy work schedule that means I often have to work in the evenings and at weekends. If I were sitting around watching television all day, or relaxing in some other way, and then were expecting Pete to do the chores after a full day's work, then I would be right to feel guilty! But this is not the case.

I think the reason I feel guilty is that I feel that I should be the one doing the supporting; not the other way around. But I am learning that what we have is actually a relationship that demonstrates aspects of what a marriage was originally designed to be – one where we support each other, one where we respect each other and the demands on each other's time, and where we seek to help each other out whenever we can.

I am still getting my head around this, and although it is becoming easier, at times I still want to take the entire burden on to myself. But I know that, if I were to do this, I would fall apart from sheer exhaustion. I am now beginning to be able to enjoy the fact that the entire burden isn't on my shoulders – there is a freedom in being able to share the load!

I am very aware of how fortunate I am to have such a supportive husband, and I am also aware that the same is not true for many women. I do understand how difficult it can be to carry the burden of responsibility and to feel alone in doing so. I know from experience how hard it is to not have the support of a loved one. Perhaps this is one reason why I find it so hard to let go now, because I felt that I carried it all for so long, and old habits die hard.

During these difficult times I found that the easiest way for me to cope was to just get on with what needed to be done, and to try to focus my thoughts on the positive things in my life. My children, my family, my friends and my relationship with God gave me more than enough reasons to keep going; they helped me find the strength to carry on when it was really tough, and enabled me to stay focused on the good things in my life.

I have been blessed to have people around me who have respected me, what I do and what I can contribute, and these people have helped me in turn to learn to value myself and what I am able to give.

I have also found it helpful to understand more about the way Jesus valued everyone around Him. This included women, children and those whom society deemed to be 'unlovable', either because they were 'sinful', sick or ritually unclean. He loved everyone, equally. He spent His time with those who needed His help, comparing himself to a doctor who had come to help the sick.[17] Jesus didn't discriminate.

Upside down values

I am not a big fan of the word 'equality' when it refers to men and women; to me it conveys the idea of something that has had to be fought for, which I don't think is a good thing. Anything that is forced, I feel, is not real and has shallow foundations.

By saying this I don't wish to devalue in any way what many women have fought for for many years; indeed, this has

---

[17] Matthew 9:12.

been very necessary in order for women to be recognised and appreciated, and I have the utmost admiration for all the women who have sacrificed so much so that we can have the freedom and respect we have today, but I think it is terribly sad that it has come at such a cost.

I prefer to consider the relationship that should exist between men and women as one of mutual respect and understanding, valuing each other for our differences as well as our similarities.

I want to think a little about God's view of men and women, and the view that I believe God would like us as human beings to have of ourselves.

Genesis 1:27 tells us that 'God created mankind in his own image, in the image of God he created them; male and female he created them.' God then blessed the man and the woman and gave *them* authority over the earth, to look after the world He had made and all the creatures in it (verse 28).

Men and women are inherently different – there is no doubt about that – and I believe this is a wonderful thing. God deliberately made us to be men and women. He didn't have to do this – He could quite easily have given the human race the ability to procreate from just one gender, but He didn't. It was a deliberate decision on God's part to create both men *and* women, so that we could complement each other, enjoy each other's differences, embrace each other's strengths, support each other's weaknesses and live together in a relationship of mutual respect and shared authority.

Men and women are, obviously, of different genders, but God is neither, and He is both. In the Bible, God is referred to as 'he', but the English language doesn't have a neutral pronoun, which is why 'he' and 'him' are used throughout.

I believe God made men and women to portray different aspects of Himself, and these are revealed as we read the Bible. In verse 2 of Psalm 91, for example, God is described as 'refuge' and 'fortress'; perhaps these would be ascribed to the 'maleness' of God's personality – strong and powerful.

In verse 4 of the same psalm, the writer says that 'He will cover you with his feathers, and under his wings you will find refuge'. To me this conveys the image of a mother hen, and might be considered to be depicting nurturing aspects of God's character, which are perhaps more feminine instincts.

Women in biblical times had very few rights. They weren't educated, and they certainly appear to have been viewed as second-class citizens. Children were viewed in the same way. They were to know their place, and were to be 'seen and not heard'. Any person with an illness or disease that made them ritually unclean was also rejected by society.

Jesus turned all this on its head. He welcomed both men and women, including *sinful* men and women. He was cross with the disciples for turning children away because He wanted to welcome them and bless them.[18] He spent much of His time with outcasts, sinners and those whom society had rejected – both men and women.

Jesus was not ashamed to associate with women, as other leaders of the time are likely to have been, and He welcomed them among His followers. He healed many women, including one who had been bleeding for 12 years. This woman was ritually unclean according to the Jewish Law, and therefore should not have come anywhere near Jesus for fear of making Him 'unclean' too. Rather than rejecting and rebuking her for touching the edge of His cloak, Jesus welcomed her and spoke kindly to her.[19] Instead of being made unclean by the woman, Jesus made her clean.

When Jesus healed the man with the withered hand, this, too, should have made Jesus unclean according to the Law. But,

---

[18] Mark 10:13-16.
[19] Luke 8:48.

once again, Jesus made him clean, while not compromising any of His own holiness and 'cleanliness'.[20]

These are just two examples of how He turned society and its values upside down.

Mary and Martha

Luke tells us of the occasion when Jesus went to the home of Mary and Martha. Martha was busy with all the preparations that had to be made, while Mary sat and listened to Jesus teaching. Presumably she was sitting among the men.

We are led to believe that Martha became quite irritated at having to do all the work herself, and asked Jesus to tell Mary to help her. Jesus' reaction here is very interesting, and very insightful. He saw that Martha was 'worried and upset about many things', and told her that 'few things are needed – or indeed only one'. Mary had chosen to spend her time with Jesus, and Jesus said that she had made the right choice.[21]

I can really relate to Martha in this story. I have a tendency to get bogged down in the practicalities of things because I want everything to function properly and run smoothly. I guess that's the perfectionist in me coming to the fore. I am not saying this isn't important – I think it is, because otherwise life would be chaos (or more chaotic than it is already!) – but I know that sometimes I just need to take some time out and listen to Jesus. I need to make sure I get my priorities in the right order. If I am spending too much time on practical things, or too much time working and not enough time with Jesus, my relationship with

---

[20] Matthew 12:9-13.
[21] Luke 10:38-42.

Him will suffer, and my relationship with Him is the most important thing in my life.

I think the other thing we can glean from this is that, whatever we do, it must be with the right motivation. Martha was cooking and making all the preparations, and I'm sure that was the right thing for her to be doing. Serving others is of immense value in the kingdom of God, and is something that Jesus himself modelled for us on many occasions.

If Martha had chosen to sit with Jesus along with Mary, who would have prepared the food? I don't know. Perhaps they would have all mucked in after Jesus had finished talking with them. What I am sure about, though, is that, if Martha had chosen to sit with Jesus too, Jesus would not have rejected her and sent her back to the kitchen. It was Martha's choice to be doing what she was doing; she wasn't following anybody's orders.

I think maybe what Jesus was trying to say to Martha was, whatever you do, do it willingly and from your heart. If you aren't doing it with the right motives, perhaps you shouldn't be doing it at all.

Again, I find this quite a challenge. Sometimes I do things because I know they need to be done, but while I do them I find myself feeling resentful and wishing that I could be somewhere else, doing something else. Is this honouring to God? I don't think so. He 'loves a cheerful giver'.[22]

Jesus' attitude to Mary is also very interesting. In the society of the day, women were not permitted to be taught the Scriptures. However, Jesus not only allowed Mary to listen to him, but He actively encouraged it. I think this says a lot about Jesus' view of women. He did not think that they were not intelligent enough to understand, neither did He consider that they were not important enough to be taught, and He didn't

---

[22] 2 Corinthians 9:7.

think that they were not entitled to have an opinion of their own. In short, He showed respect for women.

Mary Magdalene and others

Luke tells us that among Jesus' followers were a number of women whom He had healed, and that they were 'helping to support them out of their own means'.

Mary Magdalene was one of Jesus' followers, and she is described as one 'from whom seven demons had come out'.[23] We aren't told much about Mary's past. Some people believe that this Mary is the one who anointed Jesus' feet with perfume in Luke 7, but we are not told in the Bible that they were the same person. The woman who anointed Jesus' feet had 'lived a sinful life', but Jesus didn't reject her. He welcomed her, forgave her and blessed her.[24]

This tells me that Jesus is more interested in a person's heart than in what they have done. Our past is not important to Him, but our present and our future are. He looks at the heart and sees who we truly are. How many times in the gospel does He say to people, 'Your faith has saved you,' or, 'Your faith has made you well'? It is faith in Him that counts, not the things that we do. What we do and the way we live our lives should be a natural consequence of our belief and faith in him, and our love for and gratitude to him.

The Jews were God's chosen people, the ones who would be blessed by God and through whom He would bless all the nations of the world.[25] Jesus made it clear that the good news

---

[23] Luke 8:2-3.

[24] Luke 7:36-50.

[25] Genesis 12:3.

wasn't only for Jews, however, but that He came to embrace everyone who believed in him, whether Jew or Gentile. He healed the servant of a Roman centurion because he showed great faith. Indeed, Jesus said of him, 'I tell you, I have not found such great faith even in Israel.'[26]

If we look at the anointing of David as king, we see there, too, that God is more interested in a person's heart. David's father, Jesse, had eight sons, and Samuel had been told by God to anoint one of them as the next king. Seven of them were rejected by God, and the youngest – David – was the one God chose. God said to Samuel about one the older sons:

> Do not consider his appearance or his height, for I have rejected him. The Lord does not look at the things people look at. People look at the outward appearance, but the Lord looks at the heart.
> *1 Samuel 16:7*

Rahab, in the Old Testament, was a prostitute. God used her to protect the spies that Joshua sent to check out the land of Jericho before the Israelites conquered it.[27] Not only were she and her family saved from certain death as a result of her actions, but she is also recorded in the genealogy of Jesus in the first chapter of Matthew's gospel! Hebrews 11:31 tells us that, 'By faith the prostitute Rahab, because she welcomed the spies, was not killed with those who were disobedient.' God is interested in our heart, and when He sees faith there, He is able to do amazing things.

I am always encouraged by this. Although I try to live a good life, I do get it wrong sometimes. Reading passages like these helps me to understand that I don't have to be perfect for Jesus to love me or to use me.

---

[26] Luke 7:1-10
[27] Joshua 2.

All through the Bible, in both the Old and the New Testaments, we see examples of people who were saved by their faith in God, because they believed in Him and trusted Him to help them.

Embrace the extraordinary!

Life is an ongoing journey, and we never really know where we will end up. We may have an idea, but as we follow the twists and turns en route, we will inevitably be surprised at times by where we find ourselves.

As I have shared with you some of the experiences and observations of my own journey, I hope you have found them helpful and interesting. As I look back on how far I have come, I am grateful to God, to my family, to my friends, to my church family, and to all who have played a part in making my journey what it has been.

There have been difficult times and there have been easier times, and they have all played a part in making me who I am. Even the difficult times are valuable: I can learn a lot from them, and they also help me to appreciate the many good things I have and to not take them for granted.

Being self-employed and working from home, it is easy sometimes to fall into the trap of working too much, particularly now that I am studying as well. But I know how important my family and my friends are, and I try to make a conscious effort to keep things in perspective and ensure that I balance my time in the right way. I know I don't always get it right.

I know that my relationships are a gift from God. I must cherish them, nurture them and grow them, like a rare flower. They are something beautiful and, with the right amount of tender loving care, they will thrive and bring great joy and pleasure, not only to those within the relationship but to others around.

I no longer feel that I am 'less than ordinary'. What is 'ordinary' anyway? I want to live an extraordinary life, doing the extraordinary and exciting things that God has in store for me.

I believe that every single one of us has the potential to live an extraordinary life, and I hope my story has enabled you to realise that you are not 'less than ordinary' either; indeed, you, too, are an extraordinary person. You are uniquely created to fill a hole in this world that only you can fill. Your journey will be very different from mine, but I encourage you to embrace it, to step out, and to enjoy the ride!

I will give the last word to George Eliot (who, incidentally, was a woman):

> It seems to me we can never give up longing and wishing while we are thoroughly alive. There are certain things we feel to be beautiful and good, and we *must* hunger after them.[28]

---

[28] George Eliot, *The Mill on the Floss*, Book V, Chapter 1 (1860).